# Antelope Woman

*An Apache Folktale*

Retold and illustrated by
# Michael Lacapa author of *The Flute Player*

NORTHLAND PUBLISHING

Copyright © 1992 by Michael Lacapa

Cover Design by David Jenney

Text Design by Carolyn Gibbs

FIRST EDITION

SECOND PRINTING, 1993

ISBN 0-87358-543-7

Library of Congress Catalog Card Number  92-14098

Manufactured in Hong Kong by Sing Cheong

Cataloging-in-Publication Data

Lacapa, Michael.

Antelope Woman  :  an Apache folktale / retold and illustrated by Michael Lacapa.

48 p.

1st ed.

Summary:  A beautiful Apache maiden follows the mysterious young man who has come

to teach her people to respect "all things great and small" and becomes his wife.

ISBN 0-87358-543-7 (hardcover)  :  $14.95

1. Apache Indians--Legends.   [1. Apache Indians--Legends.

2. Indians of North America--Legends.]  I.  Title.

E99.A6L32     1992

[398.2]--dc20                        92-14098

CIP

AC

3-93/7.5M/0451

*To the Creator,*

*the Giver of Life, who taught us to honor*

*all things great and small.*

"Listen, my son. As we go to hunt today, let me tell you of the people who lived here long ago and why we honor all things around us, great and small.

"Here in this valley, the people lived, and among the people was a beautiful young woman, a strong worker. She knew how to gather berries early in the morning and how to gather wood for her family. She also knew how to make strong baskets. You see, she was very special.

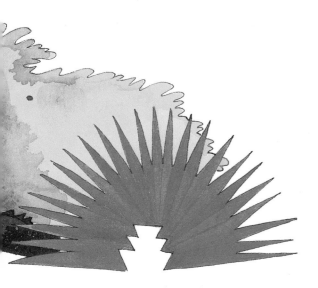

"Young men from other villages would come to see her and try to get her attention by walking in front of her with their horses, bows and arrows, and colorful shirts and shoes. But they did not interest her.

"One day, a young man who was not like the other young men came to the village. He came to talk to all the people in the village.

"He went to the men, sat down, and began telling them of ways in which to hunt and protect their families. He said, 'When hunting, remember to respect all things great and small.' In the evening, he left.

"The next morning, when the young woman got up to gather wood and berries, she saw the young man helping an elderly man make a bow. He said, 'This is how to make it stronger and, remember, as you hunt with this bow, respect all things great and small.' The older man agreed, and the young woman too. Later that evening, the young man left the village. No one knew when he left or where he had gone.

"The next day, he returned. The young woman saw him helping a woman carry water from the river. As they walked, the young man told the woman, 'We must even honor the water, for it flows down from the mountains to nourish the plants. It nourishes our brothers, the animals. It also nourishes us, the people. We must respect all things great and small.'

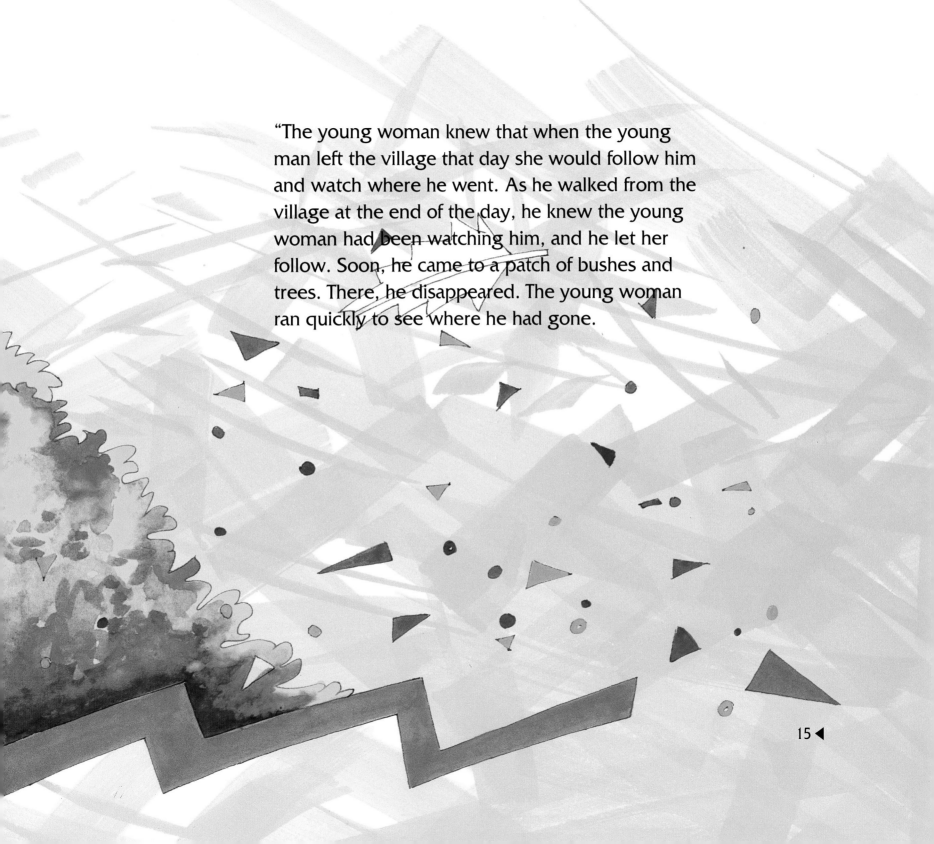

"The young woman knew that when the young man left the village that day she would follow him and watch where he went. As he walked from the village at the end of the day, he knew the young woman had been watching him, and he let her follow. Soon, he came to a patch of bushes and trees. There, he disappeared. The young woman ran quickly to see where he had gone.

"Just as she reached the trees, she saw him jump
through four hoops, and then something happened. 17 ◀

"Looking back at her, the young man nodded, but she noticed he was not a man anymore. He was an antelope. He motioned for her to follow him, and she did.

"She began to go through the hoops, one after another. As she jumped through the fourth one, she felt herself changed.

21 ◀

"Then the young man told her, 'You must come with me. I will teach you so you too can tell the people to honor all things great and small.'

"The young man and woman walked to a pool of deep water. On the far side of the water were more antelope, who began talking to the young man in a different language. For, you see, they were his people, the antelope. The young woman felt thirsty and began to drink. As she looked into the water, she saw her reflection. She was no longer a woman but an antelope. The young man said, 'You must come with me. I will show you why we must be thankful for all things.'

"Then he called to her, 'Come here quickly. Quickly!' Suddenly all of the antelope were running. They ran until they came to a patch of prickly pear cactus and then they ran through it. The young woman was surprised to find she could somehow step through the prickly pear without hurting her feet. She looked behind her and saw the coyote who had been chasing them. He looked hungry and angry because he could not get to them through the cactus. The young man said to her, 'See, we must be thankful for the sharp prickly pear because it gives us protection from those who wish to have us. It is good to honor all things great and small.'

"After the coyote left, the young woman was happy—and thankful. When the herd began running again, quickly and gracefully, she was thankful that she, too, could run and jump across the plain, through the high grass, and over bushes and small trees. Then she thought of her family. Her family! While learning about things for which to be thankful, she had forgotten her family and her people. She said to the young man, 'We must return to the people and share this knowledge with them.' The young man agreed.

29 ◄

"The next day, they returned through the hoops, were changed back into people, and entered the village. The young man carried with him many gifts—deer hides, jewelry, beads, corn, bows and arrows, and many colorful stones. He brought these gifts for the young woman's family, for he was to marry her.

"The young woman's mother was excited to see her daughter, for, you see, time had passed, and the people had been very worried about her. She told her parents that she and the young man were to be married. The family agreed by accepting his gifts. Soon the young couple married and stayed in the village.

"The people were happy, for the young man showed them many things that would help them through the long, cold winters and the hot, dry summers. He showed them ways to live and ways to learn. During this time, the young woman became pregnant and gave birth. The young man was proud of his children, a boy and a girl. But because they were twins, the people did not accept them.

"The young couple felt sad and began to talk. The young father said, 'Remember when we ran together with my family? It was special. You knew at that time it was important to honor the family. Now you must honor our family by going where we will be accepted. We are not like your people, and they do not accept us. My people will accept us because they have learned how to honor the family and all things great and small.'

"With that, the young mother agreed. She told her parents that she would have to go with her husband to his village. The people watched the young family walk to the place of the four hoops. After the young couple passed through the hoops, they were never seen again.

"Since then, we have learned to honor all things great and small. So today, my son, we honor the antelope by never hunting or killing them. For out there among the antelope are Antelope Woman and her children and they are a part of us. Now as we hunt, my son, we must be thankful to the creator, who gives us all things great and small and who teaches us to honor them all.

"Shí goshk'án dasjaá."
*(The story ends here.)*

## ACKNOWLEDGMENTS

Many thanks to Dr. Joseph Rubin, a close friend who fanned the fire of the Antelope Woman story; and to Dr. Ekkehart Malotki, for opening the door of opportunity and allowing me to step in.

Sharing and talking with Richard Sanchez and Byrd Baylor were especially helpful.

I am eternally grateful to Mom, Antonia Kessay Lacapa, from whom my desires were fed and nourished as a child. Thanks to the Home Boyz, Ron and Rondi Vinnedge, Larry and Marva Fellows.

Finally, my thanks to Kathy, Daniel, Rochelle, and Anthony, my family, who reflected love and patience during the multitude of nights, weekends, and months spent working on this book.

## ABOUT THE AUTHOR

Michael Lacapa is an award-winning author and illustrator of books for children, including *The Mouse Couple* and *The Flute Player*. Of Apache, Hopi, and Tewa descent, he gains his inspiration from traditional storytellers, while using his cultural roots and artistic training to develop stories filled with the designs and patterns found in basketry and pottery indigenous to the Southwest.

As an artist, Mr. Lacapa incorporates bold colors and varied brush strokes to reinforce the storyline in each illustration. One of many artists in his culture, he recognizes his gift as one from the Creator. "The Creator allows my hand to change the surface of paper with paint and ink, and he allows my voice to share the truth found in stories."

He currently lives in Taylor, Arizona, with his wife and three children.

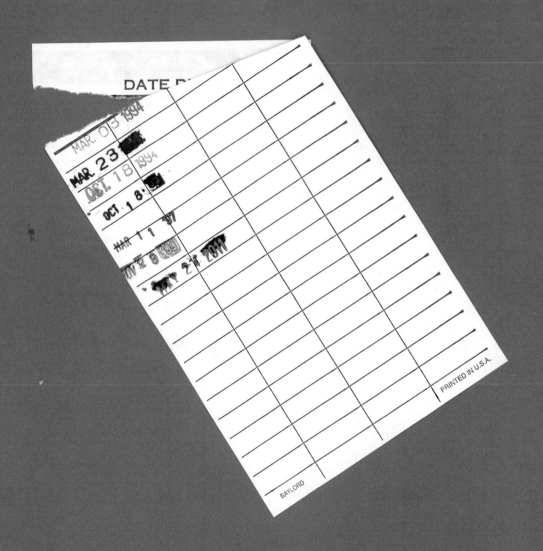